THE
HOUSE OF FALLING LEAVES

In Memoriam Frederic Lawrence Knowles
obiit Sept. 19, 1905

THE HOUSE OF FALLING LEAVES

With Other Poems

By WILLIAM STANLEY BRAITHWAITE

Author of "Lyrics of Life and Love"

LUCE ET LABORE

BOSTON

JOHN W. LUCE AND COMPANY

1908

Reprinted by Mnemosyne Publishing Co., Inc. Miami, Florida

First Mnemosyne reprinting 1969

**Reprinted from a copy in the
Fisk University Library Negro Collection.**

Copyright © 1969   Mnemosyne Publishing Co., Inc.   Miami, Florida

Library of Congress Catalog Card Number:
77-83937

Printed in the United States of America

To the Memory of
FREDERIC LAWRENCE KNOWLES

FOR courteous permission to reprint certain poems in this collection, acknowledgment is due which I hereby gratefully render, to the Editors of the following magazines: *The Century, Book News Monthly, The Christian Endeavor World, The Voice, The New England Magazine, The American Magazine,* and *The New York Times Saturday Review of Books.*

CONTENTS

[ix]

[x]

THE HOUSE OF FALLING LEAVES

I

OFF our New England coast the sea to-night
Is moaning the full sorrow of its heart:
There is no will to comfort it apart
Since moon and stars are hidden from its sight.
And out beyond the furthest harbor-light
There runs a tide that marks not any chart
Wherewith man knows the ending and the start
Of that long voyage in the infinite.

If change and fate and hapless circumstance
May baffle and perplex the moaning sea,
And day and night in alternate advance
Still hold the primal Reasoning in fee,
Cannot my Grief be strong enough to chance
My voice across the tide I cannot see?

II

We go from house to house, from town to town,
And fill the distance full of smiles and words;
We take all pleasure that our strength affords
And care not if the sun be up or down.
The way of it no man has ever known —
But suddenly there is a snap of chords
Within the heart that sounds like hollow boards, —
We question every shadow that is thrown.

O to be near when the last word is said!
And see the last reflection in the eye —
For when the word is brought our friend is dead,
How bitter is the tear that will not dry,
Because so far away our steps are led
When Love should draw us close to say Good-bye!

III

Four seasons are there to the circling year:
Four houses where the dreams of men abide —
The stark and naked Winter without pride,
The Spring like a young maiden soft and fair;
The Summer like a bride about to bear
The issue of the love she deified;
And lastly, Autumn, on the turning tide
That ebbs the voice of nature to its bier.

Four houses with two spacious chambers each,
Named Birth and Death, wherein Time joys and
    grieves.
Is there no Fate so wise enough to teach
Into which door Life enters and retrieves?
What matter since his voice is out of reach,
And Sorrow fills My House of Falling Leaves!

IV

The House of Falling Leaves we entered in —
He and I — we entered in and found it fair;
At midnight some one called him up the stair,
And closed him in the Room I could not win.
Now must I go alone out in the din
Of hurrying days: for forth he cannot fare;
I must go on with Time, and leave him there
In Autumn's house where dreams will soon grow
    thin.

When Time shall close the door unto the house
And opens that of Winter's soon to be,
And dreams go moving through the ruined
    boughs —
He who went in comes out a Memory.
From his deep sleep no sound may e'er arouse, —
The moaning rain, nor wind-embattled sea.

MY THOUGHTS GO MARCHING
LIKE AN ARMÈD HOST

MY thoughts go marching like an armèd host
  Out of the city of silence, guns and cars;
Troop after troop across my dreams they post
  To the invasion of the winds and stars.
O brave array of youth's untamed desire!
  With thy bold, dauntless captain Hope to lead
His raw recruits to Fate's opposing fire,
  And up the walls of Circumstance to bleed.
How fares the expedition in the end?
  When this, my heart, shall have old age for king
And to the wars no further troop can send,
  What final message will the arm'stice bring?
The host gone forth in youth the world to meet,
In age returns — in victory or defeat?

MATER TRIUMPHALIS

To Louise Imogen Guiney

FORESEEN in Eve's desire,
　　Foreborne in Adam's bliss,
The whim of a dream on fire
　　Has brought the world to this:
Foregone was the break of order,
　　Ere the Will was disobeyed
And the Angel at Eden's border
　　Stood with a flaming blade.

This was at the beginning —
　　What shall it be at the end!
For the first child borne in sinning
　　Will God or Nature befriend?
Eve's desire is yet burning
　　Fair women in country and town,
And Adam's bliss is turning
　　Empires and kingdoms down.

Is this the worth of a story,
  Is this the dream of a song —
A fabled blare of glory,
  This battle of right and wrong?
O sweet, fair body of woman,
  O strong, brave will of man —
Co-equal in the human,
  Unequal in the plan!

The deeds of warriors vanish,
  The words of martyrs die,
But never the heart can banish
  The drift of Helen's sigh.
Jerusalem is forsaken,
  Gomorrah is a lure —
Eve, once from her sleep awaken,
  And Adam's kiss is sure.

But God is yet the Master,
    The dramatist of the play;
If He wove an act of disaster,
    He wove an act to allay.
Deep in the dream's forebeing
    The Artist was greater than life
Who smiled at His own foreseeing
    The Virgin mother and wife.

MESSENGERS OF DREAMS

MY heart can tell them, every one,
The messengers of dreams that run
Above the tree-tops in the sun.

Whether of great or little worth
They carry the heart's desires forth
East and west and south and north.

I know the night will close them in —
And they will meet the tempest's din —
Ere they come to that far-off inn.

The inn that stands on the bourne of hope,
Where Fear and Delight together cope
For victory on a little slope.

My heart can tell them, every one,
The returning messengers that run
Above the tree-tops in the sun.

A WHITE ROAD

A WHITE road between sea and land,
　　Night and silence on either hand —
Pointing to some unknown gate
A white forefinger of fate.

I follow, I follow — I'll wend
My way on this road to the end;
Silence may keep to the sea,
On land no light shines free.

Bend low impenetrable sky —
Through your shades my road runs high:
It needs no stars to guide —
No measuring sea-tide.

I breathe the imperishable breath,
I trespass the bounds of death —
For my heart knows all the way
To the eternal day.

TO ARTHUR UPSON

HOW placidly this silent river rolls
    Under the midnight stars before our feet,
While we chaunt music of dead poets' souls
    The treasury of Time has made so sweet.
This is my Charles, O Friend! the loving nurse
Of a boy's heart who dreamed life would be worse
    Than death, if he gave not in future years
    Some few more songs to those this river bears..
Ah, here we sit, the boy's heart grown to man's —
    Westward from Cambridge, hid among the hills,
Breaks forth its source no wider than your
    hands; —
    How like our own experience it fills
Here at this point its widening banks, as we
Grow out to fill our duties, to the sea!

Here all the night is on us with its stars;
   The pregnant silence tapers to a sound;
The river's crossed with pulsing silver bars
   The distant lights reflect; upon this mound
We sit through this eternal hour of time
And read the book our souls have writ in rhyme:
   Youth's golden chapters done in poetry —
   But where this river here runs on to sea
By muddy flats, stone walls, and wharves that
      close
   The glad impulsive welcome of its home,
So henceforth shall Time write our acts in prose;
   Yea, and when God adds *Finis* to the tome,
This Dedicatory night our souls will blend,
To show, though life, true Friendship cannot
      end.

ON THE DEATH OF THOMAS BAILEY ALDRICH

(*March* 19, 1907)

I

WHAT sudden bird will bring us any cheer
　　Whose song in the chill dawn gives hope
　of Spring;
Can we be glad to give it welcoming
Though April in its music be so near?
Not while the burden of our memories bear
The weight of silence that we know will cling
About the lips that nevermore will sing
The heart of him with visions voiced so clear.

There is a pause in meeting before speech
Between men who have fed their souls with song;
The strangeness of an echo beyond reach
Cleaves silence deep for speech to pass along.
There are no words to tell the loss, but each
Of our hearts feels the sorrow deep and strong.

II

The Wondersmith in vocables is dead!
The Builder of the palaces of rhyme
Shall build no more his music out of Time.
In the deep, breathless peace to which he fled
He sits with Landor's hands upon his head
Watching our suns and stars that sink and climb
Between him and our tears' continuous chime —
Sorrowing for his presence vanishèd.

Aldrich is dead! but the glory of his life
Is in his song, and this will keep his name
Safe above change and the assaults of strife.
Poet, whose artistry, his constant aim
Kept true above defections that were rife,
Death taking him, still leaves his deathless fame.

March 20, 21, 1907.

GOLDEN MOONRISE

WHEN your eyes gaze seaward
    Piercing through the dim
Slow descending nightfall,
On the outer rim

Where the deep blue silence
Touches sky and sea,
Hast thou seen the golden
Moon, rise silently?

Seen the great battalions
Of the stars grow pale —
Melting in the magic
Of her silver veil?

I have seen the wonder,
I have felt the balm
Of the golden moonrise
Turn to silver calm.

MADAME OF DREAMS

To John Russell Hayes

I KNOW a household made of pure delight,
   That sits within a garden of quietness:
A welcomed visitor by day or night,
   I win a refuge from life's storm and stress.
Ah, here no footfalls cease and then resume,
   Nor sounds of closing doors nor creaking beams;
And throned within her favorite gold room
Amid the roses' perfume and the gloom,
   I greet my smiling hostess, Madame of Dreams.

I know not how I won so dear a friend,
   I know not of her family or her race;
Her voice is a sweet music without end
   Unfolding the wistful beauty of her face.
She has known all the world's great tragedies —
   Was at the ruins of Troy and Actium;
And her deep heart holds many memories
That are the ghosts of countless aching sighs
   Dead lovers uttered ere their lips grew dumb.

She seems so old from her experience —
  With Egypt's queen she sailed along the Nile —
She heard Demosthenes' great eloquence —
  Saw Camelot melt 'neath Arthur's golden smile.
But Time has dealt with her as with the sea,
  Whereon it leaves not any scars nor seams;
And like a bud that breaks at last to be
A faultless rose June's dews and suns decree —
  Beauty and Youth have crowned Madame of
    Dreams.

TO FIONA

DEAR little child, whose very speech
    Gives me joy beyond my heart's measure,
However far my years may reach,
    Life can offer no greater treasure.

Loveliest flower in my garden of dreams!
    Mine have been sweet like fairy stories —
But of all that have come true, it seems
    Your babyhood brought the greatest glories.

All my life long I have tried to make
    Dreams in a perfect song go winging;
I knew the wonder when you spake,
    And your life went a lyric singing.

TO FIONA

Nineteen Months Old

NOW my songs shall grow
   Sweeter, year by year,
Just because I know
   You shall read them, dear,

When your little hands,
   And your little eyes,
Babyhood expands
   Into grown-up wise.

You will ask me then,
   Reading what I write
Of my youth and then
   Song of you took flight.

Darling, I shall say —
   Just because I knew
In some future day
   You would hold them true:

" *Father wrote these songs*
  When I was a child;
Now to me belongs
  All his dreams exiled.

" *Mine is all the joy,*
  Mine are all the tears
In the heart of boy
  And the man of years."

This, my little one,
  Is what you will say,
When my songs are done,
  And my hair is grey.

But my songs I know,
  Sweeter, year by year,
From my heart will flow
  For your soul to hear —

When your little hands,
  And your little eyes,
Babyhood expands
  Into grown-up wise.

OFF THE NEW ENGLAND COAST

To John Daniel

THE earth is our Mother, but thou, thou art
    Father of us and of Time,
For all things now were not, when thou wast
    strong in thy prime.
There was silence first and then darkness, and
    under the garment of these
Was the body of thee in thy might with its infinite
    mysteries.
And God alone was aware of thy presence and
    power and form:
And out of His knowledge foresaw His will in
    thy calm and storm;
Answering unto His will he gave thee lordship
    and crown,
And bade the kingdoms of man to worship thee
    and bow down.
For earth He made out of dust for change and
    defeat in the blast —
But thee He made eternal, through æons and
    æons to last

[33]

Unmarked by sun or wind, supreme where thy
   waves are tost —
Not an inch of thy Beauty to perish, nor an
   ounce of thy Might to be lost.

II

Between the morning-star and the sea
The black night hangs disconsolately;
Winds from the gates of the east arise
And crack the silence to the skies
Through which the long grey dawn can flee
Between the morning-star and the sea.

Between closed eyelids and the sea
An echo floats continuously;
The spirit wavers ere 'tis won,
As the east pauses ere the sun
Lights the whole world up, radiantly,
Between closed eyelids and the sea.

Between the sunlight and the sea
Time hoists her sails, pulls anchor free;
The ship of Life moves on its keel —
Humanity commands the wheel
And steers for one more Hope to be
Between the sunlight and the sea.

III

The night being done
And the day begun
With the reappearance of the lordly sun,
To labor and cope
The earth gives scope,
And to every man the strength of hope.

With each new morn
There is reborn
Some effort which yesterday left forlorn;
For a little rest,
And a will to test,
Is the road that runs from worst to best.

No man is poor
Who can endure
The will to forget what is past and sure,
Of the change and fate
That participate
In defeats that passed him through last night's
    gate:

Instead he is rich,
Who can forward pitch
His breast to the front of To-day — to which
The recompense
Must yield defence,
And Time surrender the consequence.

IV

Over the world hangs the splendor of noonday,
  The winds fold their echoes away in the offing;
  Up the long coast comes a murmur of laughing
Where the little foam-waves and the sand-dunes
    play.
  Here far away from man's hating and scoffing,
  Time leads the sun home to the house of his
    dreams.

This is the way of the world in a vision —
  Hope that's alluring, and desires that follow:
  Tears that are eloquent, laughter that's hollow:
Beauty forever pursuing her mission. —
  But I care not for these, — when the seas call
    low
  Time leads the sun home to the house of his
    dreams.

Greyness of dawn cannot dull the noon's bright-
    ness,
  Shadows of even cannot mask it and darken;
  Men of the world may pass through it, nor
    hearken
Beat of its pulses that make the stars sightless.
  Triumphing out of the pause that is flightless
  Time leads the sun home to the house of his
    dreams.

This is the joy of man's heart in its dreaming:
  The midmost heaven of all his desire —
  Farther than noon lo! the sun mounts no higher,
And Love in man's life is his noon-sun a-beaming.
  Clouds full of silence, and sky full of fire,
  Time leads the sun home to the house of his
    dreams.

OCTOBER XXIX, 1795

Keats' Birthday

TIME sitting on the throne of Memory
   Bade all her subject Days, the past had
   known,
Arise and say what thing gave them renown
Unforgetable. ' Rising from the sea,
I gave the Genoese his dream to be; '
' I saw the Corsican's Guards swept down; '
' Colonies I made free from a tyrant's crown; ' —
So each Day told its immortality.

And with these blazing triumphs spoke one voice
Whose wistful speech no vaunting did employ:
' I know not if 'twere by Fate's chance or choice
I hold the lowly birth of an English boy;
I only know he made man's heart rejoice
Because he played with Beauty for a toy.'

SONG OF A SYRIAN LACE SELLER

To Edward F. Burns

ON the sidewalk by the busy flow
　　Of peoples passing to and fro —
Where the wan winter sunlight falls
Across the grey gates of St. Paul's,
A woman of an alien race
Stands with a tray of fancy lace.

Swarthy of skin with raven hair,
A daughter of the Orient there,
Wearing her native costume yet
Of woven shawl and long head net —
And the long Syrian sunrise
Looking out from her curtained eyes.

The curious, intricate designs
Of every lace in faultless lines
Of ancient symbols she has made,
Turning her country's lore to trade:
The Orient's mystic sorcery,
In this far land across the sea.

Out of the Common sharp and fleet
The cold winds blow across the street;
And their shrill voices seem to say:
Symbols and dreams have passed away —
And our wise western world decries
All their lost hidden mysteries.

NYMPHOLEPSY

To Burton Kline

THE slanting gleam upon the wing
  Of a swift-darting lark that flies;
A sudden shadow lengthening
Up the hill-side till it dies
Melted by the burning sun;
A star that shoots across the night,
The dews dissolving on the rose —
Ah, to see perfection won,
Beauty unfolded to the sight, —
And lose it, — lose it, when it goes.

I know that half our hopes are vain, —
Our finite ears pretend to catch
Beyond the stars a spheral strain;
Our Sentinel-souls forever watch
For that dim Spy they never stop;
We make our bodies clean and pure,
We fill our minds with lore and creed, —
Yet long before the curtains drop
The tired flesh cannot endure —
And much of knowledge do we need.

Out of the twofold heavenly plan,
The mystical, creative will
Wrought forth the fine achievement Man —
Perfect, and yet imperfect still;
The dust beaten into shape
Is flesh artistic, hue and line —
Splendid, superb Masterpiece;
And closed therein from escape
As the sap within the vine,
The Soul that gives the dust increase.

Now which one shall I strive to turn
To life's best usage while I stay
Where suns and winds may touch and burn
Flesh — and faith and creed o'erlay
The soul? Must they be separate
In a world that nourishes both
To perfection's destined end?
Must my soul carry a dead weight
And stunt my flesh's imperial growth,
And thwart the *Inspiration's* trend?

TO DANTE GABRIEL ROSSETTI

GREETINGS, Master, take from me
Where thou art, beyond, above
Imminent touch of earth and sea.
  May thy spirit there approve
  This oblation of my love
    Unto thee,
  Sent from where I be and move.

How can death divide and keep —
  Though it conquers sight and sound —
Silences so wide and deep
  Neither Life nor Death can bound?
  In a circle winding round
    Wake and sleep,
  Souls that search and sweep are found.

I salute thee, and rejoice,
    Master, whom our hearts now own
Thine, as the one faultless voice
    In the praise of Beauty blown
    Since Keats' lips were turned to stone,
        Ears from noise
    Of a world whose choice is known.

Unto Beauty thou didst wed
    Music, pure and absolute,
Till men's hearts agreed and said
    Thou didst master Shelley's lute —
    Time no longer can dispute,
        Laurelled head,
    Thy long memoried repute.

Subtle shapen melodies,
    Thou, my Master, bidst arise,
Colored as the autumn trees,
    Tremulous with sudden sighs,
    How God's magic underlies
        Earth and seas
    Secret sounds like these comprise.

APRILIAN RHAPSODY

STRAIGHT in the heart of the April meadows,
  Straight in the dream in the heart of you;
Deep in the glory of gleams and shadows,
  Flame and gossamer, green and blue —

Out of the nowhere east from yonder,
  Out of the presences felt and seen,
Filled with the first unremember'd wonder,
  Radiant with the memory of last year's green —

Straight in the heart of the April meadows,
  Straight in the dream in the heart of you —
Spring — in the glory of gleams and shadows,
  Flame and gossamer, green and blue!

A SONG OF LIVING

To Dr. Marcus F. Wheatland

IT is so good to be alive:
To have deep dreams: to greatly strive
Through the day's work: to dance and sing
Between the times of sorrowing —
To have a clear faith in the end
That death is life's best, trustful friend.

To be alive: to hear and see
This wonderful, strange pageantry
Of earth, in which each hour's session
Brings forth a new unknown procession
Of joys: stars, flowers, seas and grass
In ever new guise before me pass.

To have deep dreams: ah me, ah me!
To bring far things close by to see;
To have my voyaging soul explore
Beyond my body's ponderous door.
To make my love from a thousand graces,
Seen in a thousand women's faces.

To greatly strive: perform my share
Of work: for the world grows more fair
To him who measures Time and Fate
By what his laboring days create —
For work is the voice that lifts to God
The adoration of the sod.

To dance and sing: my body's praise
For being fair in many ways.
It hath no other voice than this
To thank God for a moment's bliss —
When art and heaven together trust
Joy to the perfection of the dust.

Times of sorrowing: yea, to weep:
To wash my soul with tears, and keep
It clean from earth's too constant gain,
Even as a flower needs the rain
To cool the passion of the sun,
And takes a fresh new glory on.

To have clear faith: — through good or ill
We but perform some conscious will
Higher than man's. The world at best
In all things doth but manifest
That God has set his eternal seal
Upon the unsubstantial real.

AVE AND VALE

OH far away across the beach
   The mist is in the sunset,
And dreams lie low
   In the silence of the foam;
Beyond the dim horizon
   Where the creeping darkness pauses
I hear the grey winds calling
   And they lead desire home.
     O Ave to the evening star,
       And Vale to the setting sun;
     And a deep, deep sea across the bar
       Where the grey winds call and run.

Oh far across the hope of speech
  A doubt is on desire,
And Love lies low
  In the pauses of my heart;
My speech and silence hovers
  On the verge of phantom futures,
While I watch the morrows dawning
  And the yesterdays depart.
    O Ave to the evening star,
      And Vale to the setting sun;
    And a deep, deep sea across the bar
      Where the grey winds call and run.

HOC ERAT IN VOTIS

I'LL leap to your desire
  With a flight more swift than light,
Though your soul should be a fire,
And mine, a moth in the night.

I'll leap to your desire
As the lark does to the sun,
Though it can fly no higher
Than the topmost clouds may run.

I'll leap to your desire —
And I pray God night and day,
To set your soul on fire
And burn my dreams away.

IN THE PUBLIC GARDEN

August, 1904

THE illumined fountain flashed in the pond,
It was purple, and green, and white, —
You and I in the crowd, and beyond,
The shining stars and night.

Beyond were the shining stars and the night, —
And near was the fountain at play.
— But ah, the dreams that have taken flight,
And never come home to stay.

RAIN IN SUMMER

THE afternoon grew darkening from the
    west;
A hush fell on the air, and in the trees;
The huddled birds pronounced their prophecies;
The flowers bent their heads as if to rest
Now that the tide of the sun's golden seas
In one long wave swept off the earth's wide breast.
Up sprung deft shadowy patterns by degrees,
And nature's face her soul made manifest.

Lo, in the instant, slant, like a hanging string
Of silver glass beads, pendant from the clouds
The rain descends! Leaves sing, and wavering
The tall lithe grasses dance in separate crowds.
I stand and let my soul commune, it knows
The mystery that calls it from its close.

THE ETERNAL SELF

To Vere Goldthwaite

THIS earth is but a semblance and a form —
An apparition poised in boundless space;
This life we live so sensible and warm,
Is but a dreaming in a sleep that stays
About us from the cradle to the grave.
Things seen are as inconstant as a wave
That must obey the impulse of the wind;
So in this strange communicable being
There is a higher consciousness confined —
But separate and divine, and foreseeing.

Our bodies are but garments made of clay
That is a smothering weight upon the soul —
But as the sun, conquering a cloudy day,
Our spirits penetrate to Source and Goal.
That intimate and hidden quickening
Bestowing sense and color with the Spring,
Is felt and known and seen in the design
By unsubstantial Self within the portal
Of this household of flesh, that doth confine
Part of the universally immortal.

Beyond the prison of our hopes and fears,
Beyond the undertow of passion's sea —
And stronger than the strength earth holds in
    years,
Lives man's subconscious personality.
O world withheld! seen through the hazy drift
Of this twilight of flesh, when sleep shall lift
I shall go forth my own true self at last,
And glory in the triumph of my winning
The road that joins the Future and the Past,
Where I can reach the Ending and Beginning!

THE HOUSE OF DEATH

LO, a house untenanted
   Stands beside the road of Time;
They who lived there once, have fled
   To some other house and clime.

Towers pointing to the sky
   With long shadows on the ground,
Never shade a passerby,
   Never echo back a sound.

AT NEWPORT

Sunrise: Bateman's Point

HERE'S the land's end, just discerned
By the sheer fall, where the sea below
Runs less wild since the tide has turned,
And daybreak lingers weird and low.

Between the dawn and hovering night,
On the grey sea-roof of the earth,
A crimson circle lifts in sight
And Time gives day eternal birth.

Sunset: On the Beach

I hear across the murmuring sea
The sunset cannon's sullen boom,
Whose distant dying echoes flee
Before the silence of the gloom.

The long pale shadows creep along
The dunes and over the water's verge;
A dusky sea-mist rises up
Above whose veil the ships emerge.

I know full soon the night will come,
And one shall find me waiting near:
Our hands will touch, our lips grow dumb,
And dreams steal on us unaware.

SIC VITA

HEART free, hand free,
  Blue above, brown under,
All the world to me
  Is a place of wonder.
Sun shine, moon shine,
  Stars, and winds a-blowing,
All into this heart of mine
  Flowing, flowing, flowing!

Mind free, step free,
  Days to follow after,
Joys of life sold to me
  For the price of laughter.
Girl's love, man's love,
  Love of work and duty,
Just a will of God's to prove
  Beauty, beauty, beauty!

A SONG OF THE SIXTH MONTH

GLAD, mad, and a bit sad too —
Face o' the rose in the eye of the sun;
God has dreamed and his work is done —
June's on the world, heigh-ho!

See how the greenish shadow raises
Patterns on the sun's flood of golden blazes
Round a pink, slim girl knee-deep in daisies.

What is this slow full sense of Time!
This great armada of chirp and song,
That are as a host of sails that throng
Across June's tidal sea of rhyme.

Buttercups and daisies, sing low, sing high —
Age is a fable, death is a lie —
And June's too good to tell us why!

FROM THE CROWD

I WAS captive to a dream —
And only vague forms went by;
And the tumult was the sigh
Of the sea at the end of a stream.

The clangor of cars in the street,
Darkness and clouds overhead,
And out of the lights that spread
The crowds that part and meet.

As the foam of a wave will mark
The night with a shining track,
A girl's pale face turned back
Crossing the street in the dark.

It was only a second's glance,
But my soul leaped out to her:
I felt my shaken memories stir
The dreams of an ancient trance.

LOVE LEADS HOME

NOW that all the twilight glimmers through
    the lane,
As of old, wandering, dreaming let us go;
Living so, tenderly, youth and love again,
Bringing back the past, dear, known unto us
    twain —
Tasting the happiness that we used to know.

Youth went from us long ago, fading like the
    foam
That a ship passing leaves trailing on the sea;
Seemingly youth may die, hopes may stray and
    roam:
Faithful hearts kept true and young will Love
    lead home —
Home to his first dwelling-place in the heart of
    thee.

THE FULL HOPE

LORD of my life before whose will I yield
Lo! I withdraw the barriers of my pride;
Let my heart swell a windless evening tide
Till all the marshland of my past's concealed;
Let stillness in my ecstasy be sealed
Deep as the swelling sea is deep and wide;
Lord of my life, where all my dreams abide,
Take me into thy dwelling who am healed.

Ah, Love! we shall dwell here for ever more —
In this great dwelling of our Hope fulfilled;
Ever the past behind us, and before
The golden future. What the gods have willed
Of good or bad to enter at the door,
We shall dwell here until our hearts are stilled.

A LITTLE WHILE BEFORE
FAREWELL

"A little while before farewell."—WILLIAM MORRIS

A LITTLE while before farewell
 What shall time say our lives befel
Between the summons and the hour?
Shall it be like a red rose-flower
Whose perfume is remembered bliss:
While thus in silence our souls kiss,
With no sad words to break the spell!

With no sad words to break the spell
A little while before farewell!
Only the longing in your eyes
To comfort me in Paradise.
And there behind the silences
I know the world's forgetfulness
Can change not, eyes that speak so well.

Can change not, eyes that speak so well
Where my love lives imperishable.
And passionate words can say no more:
Nor tears show grief is oversore:
But just your sad eyes — O how strange
The loneliness! the sudden change!
A little while before farewell!

A little while before farewell:
How quick Time runs to strike the knell.
When the dim curtain covering me
Comes down from great Eternity —
O then, my love, let there be heard
One never-ending sigh and word —
The low-breathed, whispered, long farewell!

TO BEAUTY

O MISTRESS of the world! Heaven's own
    dear child!
Priestess of Joy, and things that holy are;
Under thy smile men's hearts are reconciled,
    And after thy light, they follow, as a star
      Follows the moon across the tide
      A constant wooer at its side.
    And I will follow, follow thee so far
      Across the tide of life, and will adore
      And worship thee in visions evermore.

O Maiden of shy innocence I say
    Thou art too fair to live in widowhood;
Since Keats, thy lover, sleeps in Roman clay,
    For thee to be forsaken were not good.
      I fain would be thy wooer,
      Thou canst not find one truer,
    For I will love thee in whatever mood
      Thy sensitive and most delicate soul
      Doth on my spirit work its sweet control.

And it shall nevermore be truly said
  The glory of the world hath passed away;
Ah, no! the heart of dreams shall raise its head
  And Poesy again will hold her sway.
    Oh, give me power to teach
    The wonder of thy speech,
  And give thy heavenly message to our day:
    For the barren hearts of men have need
    Of the humane influence of thy creed.

SONG: TO-DAY AND TO-MORROW

TO-DAY and to-morrow, and the days that
    come after,
Springtime and summer and two seasons more;
The night full of tears and the day full of laughter,
    And dreams that come in and go out of the
    door.
O Time that is fleeting too fast for our capture,
    While the heart of our dreams beholds it pass
    by —
The yearning and burning, the desire and the
    rapture,
    Till we home to the earth and we home to the
    sky.

O harvest of dreams! when the sowing is over
And fulfilment of growth gives over all plying —
Ah, down the long sunset of life the heart-rover
  Turns twilight to weeping and darkness to
    sighing.
We gather the harvest of dreams and we store
    them
  Deep down in our hearts for the hunger that
    craves
When springtime and summer, — the laughter
    that bore them,
  Sails away like a ship that we watch on the
    waves.

LATE AUGUST

CHANGE of heart in the dreams I bear —
  Green leaf turns to brown;
The second half of the month is here,
  The days are closing down.

Love so swift to up and follow
  The season's fugitive,
If thou must, make rapture hollow,
  But leave me dreams to live.

Change of heart! O season's end!
  Time and tide and sorrow!
I care not what the Fates may send,
  Here's to ye, goodmorrow!

MALAGUEÑA

To Isabel Ward Carter

I HAVE named you Malagueña,
            Malagueña, Malagueña —
Though your eyes have never burned me,
Nor your lips have spoke, and turned me
            In a whirl of mad delight.
But the many stars that whisper
            In the night,
And the vagrant winds that lisper
            Through the day,
In the music of my dreams have learned to play,
            Malagueña, Malagueña!

All things name you, Malagueña,
            Malagueña, Malagueña —
Birds that sing in rangeless rapture,
And the glory that we capture
            From the coronated rose:
All the passion in the ocean's
            Ebbs and flows;
Ah, they fill me with emotions
            Naught can tame,
When I seek you in the shadow of a name,
            Malagueña, Malagueña!

[73]

When I meet you, Malagueña,
          Malagueña, Malagueña —
Shall we stop and gaze in wonder?
Nay, like winds that meet in thunder
          We will close in tight embrace,
And my kisses flash like lightning
          On your face;
Then our souls will feel the tightning
          Each to each,
Till remoulded into one they break in speech,
          Malagueña, Malagueña!

SONG: AS A NEW-MADE BRIDE

AS a new-made bride at the altar-stair,
 I have given my life for good or ill,
To Song, my bridegroom: a mated pair
 The bride shall do the bridegroom's will.

And we'll keep house as never before
 Was household kept on the hill of dreams,
Where Beauty will be a sign on the door
 From which Joy gleams.

UNDER THE STARS

I TAKE my soul in my hand,
  I give it, a bounding ball
(Over Love's sea and land),
  For you to toss and let fall
At command.

Dear, as we sit here together —
  Silence and alternate speech,
Dreams that are loose from the tether,
  Stars in an infinite reach
Of dark ether:

Over and under and through
  Silence and stars and the dreams,
How my emotions pursue,
  With a still passion that teems
Full of you.

O what can the stars desire,
  And what can the night fulfil,
Of a thousand thoughts on fire
  That burns on my soul's high hill
Like a pyre.

Does the flame leap upward, where
    God feels — and heat makes human,
Pity, in His heart — a snare
    To win worship for a woman
Unaware?

If He made all Time for this,
    O beloved, shall we not dare
To crown His dream with a kiss,
    While each new-born star makes fair
Night's abyss?

TEARS

I SAW the picture of your face woven in the
    rain;
All day long the rain fell, — fell into my soul;
I knew your heart last night was like music full
    of pain,
And from your wistful eyes I saw the sad tears
    roll.

Oh, silent are the heavy clouds, and silent is the
    heart,
And silence clothes the dreams that hold the
    future years;
But musical are raindrops, and eyes that droop
    apart
To let the music of your soul come flowing through
    your tears.

SONG

FAILURE is a crown of sorrow,
  Success a crown of fears —
From the Book of Life we borrow
  Leaves to turn the years.

Art is but a joy divine,
  God says yea or nay —
Love alone is worth the time,
  Live it as we may.

A VISIT TO OAK - LODGE

To Nixon Waterman

THE Heights of Arlington were wrapped in
    snow;
And over all the carmine sunset flush,
Gave nature's face a woman's love-lit blush,
As if her heart dreamed of the spring below;
So high your house, dear friend, I seemed to
    grow
Up to the evening star, where in the hush
Of twilight, I did feel the pulses brush
My soul, rising from the city that we know.

At last I reached your door — you welcomed me
With your warm genial smile and close hand-
    shake,
And gave me greetings to your company —
Your friends, whom you made mine for friend-
    ship's sake.
And there before your blazing logs did we
Soon hear the voice of dreams upon us break.

SONG: THE TRAIL OF STARS

WHEN mortals tread the trail of stars,
    High is the heart, O high:
For all things else are of the earth,
    But Love is of the sky.

The trail they tread is a path of dreams,
    Where Love a-journeying goes
To a garden beyond the gates of night
    Where blooms a flower Love knows.

THOMAS WENTWORTH HIGGINSON

For His Eighty-third Birthday

BENEATH the bare-boughed Cambridge elms
     to-day
  Time takes no flight in his unwintered heart;
  Where fourscore years and three came to depart,
The vision shines that cannot burn away.
In perils of change his voice is still our stay,
  Who kept the true direction from the start.
  He knew no deed born from his thoughts apart—
And held his pen Truth's summons to obey.

O reverend head, take this our crown of praise,
  On this, thy Birthday, hallowed by our love;
A soldier's honor and a poet's bays;
  In public heed thy virtues held to prove—
Though long, we wish thee longer, length of days,
  To lead us up the heights where we would move.

WILLIAM DEAN HOWELLS

For His Seventieth Birthday

SEVENTY *years!* The magic of youth
Wrought in the stern old age of Truth.
Seventy years has Howells grown
Through the infinite seen to the finite known.
Shed in his wonder of things commonplace
A mind of wisdom, a heart of grace;
Building life on the faith he had
That the world was neither too good nor bad.
Years has he reached of the liberal span
Vouchsafed the journey of mortal man:
And keeping good trust of soul and heart
The Master built him a palace of Art.

" *Open my heart and you shall see*
Grav'd inside of it, ' Italy.' "
Open his heart and read inside,
" *America* " — writ with a passionate pride.
And this one symbol of hope and strife
Wove to his vision the magic of life.
At the end of a journey of seventy years
The painter who drew its joys and fears,
Its shape of body, its essence of soul,
The ways it travels to reach its goal —
Stands to-day in the glories they shed,
The laurel of greatness on his head.

The Master at Seventy! He it is knows
The way of perfection hid deep in a rose!

THE SHEPHERD OF THE FLOCK
OF DREAMS

HE calls them out with a musical shout
   From the folds that are lying nowhere;
And up they climb to the meadows of Time
   Through the seasons of the slow year.
With bleat, bleat, bleat, on the road they beat,
   On the great highways of vision,
Where I hear them knock, the long white flock,
   With a rhythmical precision.

He follows them forth who values their worth
   For the clothing of man's desire;
And he makes no claim for pelf or fame,
   For he's far too rich to aspire.
His kingdom lies in the long sunrise
   Of life, where the nations arose,
And he gathers his sheep from the fields of sleep
   Where the hopes of the world repose.

THE FIRST BORN

MY little babe was two hours old!
   I came in from the wind and rain —
The summons gave me joy and pain —
More wonder than my heart could hold.

The winter afternoon was dim —
   A faint light shone across the bed;
   My wife with one dear arm outspread
Was holding the little life of him.

There on the threshold where I stood
   I had no wish to speak or move:
   For there God's presence did approve
This Mary of the Sisterhood.

LA BELLE DE DEMERARA

HER face was a fair olive hue;
   Eyes like a tropic night when dew
Makes the air heavy to the sea's rim;
Figure like a willow, subtle, slim,
That had the grace of a young queen;
Hair, as the Empress Josephine
Fashioned, when Paris bowed to her:
— La belle de Demerara.

I see it all as in a dream:
Georgetown's seawall, where the stream
Of Quality flows; among them moves
She, whom the city's pride approves,
What beauty gave and virtue crowned
When music charmed their lips to sound
This name their hearts bestowed on her,
— La belle de Demerara.

Sir Francis Hincks, at Government House
On a gala night before her bows;
Out from England on duty sent
The Colonel of the regiment
Glides with her in the stately dance;
And in her soft vivacious glance
Chief-Justice Beaumont bends to her:
— La belle de Demerara.

O Poet who sang of Dorothy Q. ;
I have a Great-Grandmother too,
Born in a British colonial place,
Sent to learn Parisian grace;
Who won all hearts in her demesne
By the Caribbean's warm blue sheen:
And large is the debt I owe to her,
— La belle de Demerara.

THE ANNUNCIATION OF THE VIRGIN

AS one who hath been dreaming all night
    long —
Some blissful, sweet, but dim foreboding dream,
Wherein the soul hath kissed some joy supreme
But knows not whence nor whither, sight or
    song —
Mary awoke 'midst her lone chamber's throng
Of chanting silences. Her soul did seem
Aware — as earth is at the dawn's first gleam —
Of strange primordial moods it gropes among.

With the day's full-blown rose of light she knew
Her dreams had been her marriage-bed with God;
Her soul now trembled in its nakedness
Before the Bridegroom: while her heart lived
    through
The consecrating, tender period
Till she should hold her Child with a caress.

GOLDEN HAIR

ONCE I made a little poem out of golden
    hair,
I put it in a dream and sent it to a rose;
And in the early dawn when I walked the garden
    fair,
I saw you, dear, before you went as every shadow
    goes.

O golden is the web o' the sun, golden is the
    sea,
And golden is the rose's heart that makes the
    garden fair —
All golden is the shadow that's in the heart of me,
And golden is the buried dream shrouded in golden
    hair.

GREY DAWN

THE grey dawn creeps on a shadowed sea,
    And the morning-star is a ghostly beam;
And or ever the sun lifts silently —
    O Love! was it a dream?

I felt you come like the light at dawn,
    I opened my soul to envelop the gleam;
Ah, the Memory stays, though the day is gone —
    O Love! was it a dream?

IN THE ATHENAEUM LOOKING OUT ON THE GRANARY BURY-ING GROUND ON A RAINY DAY IN NOVEMBER

HERE in this ancient, dusty room
   Filled with the rain-washed chill and gloom,
The wistful books stand 'round in hosts —
Familiar friends of forgotten ghosts
Who sleep in their narrow beds below
When daylight walks, and by them go
The unremembering city throng.
Here where dust and silence belong
I feel their presence in each nook
As if they too would stand and look
With me, out where the motley city lies,
With timid, unrecollecting eyes.

I feel the damp creep round my heart
Because my thoughts have grown a part
Of the infinite, ancient sense of pain
Echoing voices in the rain.
How long its unassuaging cry
Has filled man's memory with a sigh
When wind and rain among bare trees
Has made even joy feel ill at ease!
Joy! — where that tortuous winding coil
Of slaves to duty, sweat and toil —
Does joy dwell there? this monotone
Of rain is far more dumb of groan.

How old the world is — yet I think
No man has yet had his full drink
Of joy, while life flowed in his veins
Or disillusion racked his brains.
How like a picture shadow-bound
That street is 'cross the burial ground!
And from this room those forms out there
Are not so real as ghosts in here.

AS SILENT THROUGH THE WORLD
SHE GOES

AS silent through the world she goes
Companioned by a withered rose,
Where nothing is, but all things seem
The heavy will of a ghostly dream:

Even so she knows not life from death,
Nor words from music's golden breath;
The wind's moan is the sea-moan's heart,
And Love from Grief dwells not apart.

ENIGMAS

THE joy of the world is in a man's strength,
The sorrow of the world in a woman's tears;
Beauty lives and dies in a second's length,
And Time rolls on the years.

The battles of the world are in a man's dream,
The altars of the world in a woman's eyes;
Out of Eden follows one long far gleam
Till the last slow sunset dies.

SIR WALTER RALEIGH

HE heard the four winds and the seven seas,
  And voices inland under alien stars,
And drove ambition like auroral cars
Striking the hill-tops when the darkness flees.
Vain in his dreams, but brave in his vanities;
No carpet-knight yet versed in parlor wars;
And half a rogue when honesty debars
The desire to take the prize his fancy sees.

And yet he knew the silences of speech —
The leaf-heard utterance of April rains;
The echoes in the twilight out of reach
Beyond the dim horizon where it wanes.
And like the distant sea-wash on the beach
He sang a few sad tender lyric strains.

ON BLAKE'S "SONGS OF INNOCENCE"

IF thou hast ever heard on a May morn
  Within a leafy wood the wild birds sing,
And felt thy soul take joy in marvelling
How in such little creatures could be born
That pure melodious concert of the dawn —
Then thou dost know the ecstasies that wing
From pulse and passion when a dewy thorn
Is breaking from a rose-bud blossoming.

Such joy gave he, who sang the innocence
Of childhood — Blake, who was more child than
    man
In that grave wonder of his reverence
Unto which God revealed the visional plan
Of His Eternal Life : — the evidence
Smote him as Moses' rod — and music ran.

THE BOOK OF LOVE

I HOLD the book of life in my hands
When I hold your face, and press your lips
To my lips in a kiss, and touch all lands
In a thousand dreams that sail as ships,
Out of my soul across your soul
To the ends of the world you keep,
Between each shadowy golden goal
Of your eyes, where the kingdoms sleep.

Shall I ever read the history through,
And learn the dates of wars and kings —
How nations fell and rose and grew?
Ah, life's too short for smaller things
When your face is mine — the world itself,
Of past and future and present in one;
A book God wrote for my heart's own shelf,
And bound in the bindery of the sun.

TO LAURENCE HOPE

ALL the world of deep desire loves your
    song,
Touched of joy by starlight when the moon hangs
    low;
Filled with all the odors that arise and throng
All the secret memories delight can know.
Like your bulbuls singing when the dusk's in
    bloom
How your music stirs us till our joys make pain —
Pain the flower of passion's most tender doom,
Sum of all that life may lose and death may gain.
For the dreams you gave to music, sure and strong,
All the world of deep desire loves your song.

First in you the poetess, throned high and
    crowned
In the soul of us who mate a dream to rhyme;
We who wander strangely in the lure you've wound
Flowerful 'round the passions you have made
    sublime.
Was there ever poetess since Sappho sang
Who could match the fever of your pulsing blood?
Love that drew from the harp of life joy and pang,
How your playing rose and filled our hearts to
    flood;
We, your singing brothers, now chaunted and found
First in you the poetess, throned high and crowned.

THIS IS MY LIFE

TO feed my soul with beauty till I die;
  To give my hands a pleasant task to do;
To keep my heart forever filled anew
With dreams and wonders which the days supply;
To love all conscious living, and thereby
Respect the brute who renders up its due,
And know the world as planned is good and
    true —
And thus — because there chanced to be an *I!*

This is my life since things are as they are:
One half akin to flowers and the grass:
The rest a law unto the changeless star.
And I believe when I shall come to pass
Within the Door His hand shall hold ajar
I'll leave no echoing whisper of *Alas!*

KINGDOMS AND HEIRS

UNDER the round blue sky,
　　Over the wide green sea,
Where the sun-robed hours fly,
　　The starred silences flee:

Where birth comes down in song,
　　And death goes up in tears —
Are the kingdoms that belong
　　To dreams' uncrownèd heirs.

TO ROY ROLFE GILSON

YOU asked me out to spend the day with
    you:
How quick it passed across the face of heaven —
And yet it does not pass from out our hearts;
But in the valley of our memories
Stands as a twilight in a valley stands
Between the day and night — a moveless joy.

WHITE MAGIC: AN ODE

Read at the Centenary Celebration of the Birth of John Greenleaf Whittier at Faneuil Hall, Dec. 17, 1907

WHITE magic of the silences of snow!
    Over the Northern fields and hills, the moon
Spreads her veil o'er the wizardry below;
Amongst the ruined tree-tops is a croon
Of the long vanished populace of Spring;
    There is a glory here
Where the lone farmhouse windows, glimmering
Across the snow-fields, warm the chilly air.
Peace is upon the valley like a dream
    By Merrimac's swift stream,
Where his pure presence made the earth so fair.

Time cannot tarnish the glory of the hills:
Tides cannot wear the immaterial winds
To outworn voids where no loud echo fills
The long beach-comber which the sea unbinds;
The moon shall light the sun ere these things be;
      But sooner our glad hearts
Know not darkness from sunlight on the sea
Ere from the lips of Memory departs
Thought or speech unpraiseful of Whittier's life,
      White magic of song and strife —
Strife for the right — Song for a sake not art's.

In the rough farmhouse of his lowly birth
The spirit of poetry fired his youthful years;
No palace was more radiant on earth,
Than the rude home where simple joys and
    tears
Filled the boy's soul with the human chronicle
      Of lives that touched the soil.
He heard about him voices — and he fell
To dreams, of the dim past, 'midst his daily toil;
Romance and legend claimed his Muses' voice
      Till the heroic choice
Of duty led him to the battle's broil.

Song then became a trumpet-blast; he smote
The arrogance of evil in the State;
The indignation of his music wrote
A flaming wrath in councils of debate.
'Twas passion for the justice of God's word —
    Man's common heritage
Fulfilled in the high name of Brotherhood.
The oracle and prophet of his age,
He led men doubtful between wrong and right
        Through Song to see the light,
And smite the evil power with their rage.

He helped to seal the doom. His hope was peace
With the great end attained. Beyond his will
Fate shaped his aims to awful destinies
Of vengeful justice; — now valley and hill
Groaned with the roar of onset; near and far
        The terrible, sad cries
Of slaughtered men pierced into sun and star;
Beyond his will the violence — but the prize
Of Freedom, blood had purchased, won to God
        His praise that all men trod
Erect, and clothed in Freedom, 'neath the skies.

Let thanks be ours for this great passion in him;
And praise be our remembrance of his trust;
Blessings that no compromise could win him,
Like Ichabod, to soil his glory in the dust.
Let ours be, too, his spirit of forgiving:
  We can but master fate
By the sure knowledge of our brothers' living —
Won by matching his virtues, not his hate.
Let the white radiance of his Inward Light
  Be to us, step and sight
Up the steep road of life to Heaven's gate.

ON REVISITING NEWPORT BEACH

February 29, 1908

ONCE more I stand upon these sands, and gaze
Across the open sea.   Five winters' suns
Divide that other presence of me here,
When up the windy crescent of this beach
I walked in rapt communion of farewell.
I leave the world behind me now — forget
My late and feverish intercourse with life
And its mixed motives of the city street:
Circumstance like a garment I've cast off
And bring my naked soul for your apparel,
O sands and waves and unconfinèd winds!
O sands! whose separate grains vast worlds con-
    dense;
O winds! whose wings do beat the discs of suns;
O mutable and everlasting sea!
Thou whose being wast mother of time and man —
I stand before you naked for your dreams
To clothe my soul with Hope and Strength and
    Light.

OFF-SHORE

LOOK out across the blue-green sea,
   Look thither where the blue glooms lie —
Beyond the bourne of mystery,
   Between the sea-rim and the sky.
Oh look — and look across the deep
   Sundering, indivisible flood —
Secretive as the doom of sleep
   That falls on man's ancestral blood:

Look out and gaze from vanished eyes
   That longed for home from Tyrian ships;
Look out from ruined destinies
   That burn behind the blood's eclipse;
Look from the stare when Adam saw
   God spread Creation at his feet;
As Moses, when the Stones of Law
   God gave him where the whirlwinds meet:

Look out across the blue-green sea,
    Look thither where the blue glooms lie —
There still is Canute's mystery,
    And mocking Plato's inner eye.
Oh look with Shakespeare's teeming brain,
    And look with Voltaire's biting scorn —
Behold the sudden rush of rain —
    The miracle's unborn!

*L*ORD *of the mystic star-blown gleams*
  Whose sweet compassion lifts my dreams;
Lord of life in the lips of the rose
That kiss desire; whence Beauty grows;
Lord of the power inviolate
That keeps immune thy seas from fate;
Lord of the indestructible dew
Fresh, as the night the first rose drew
Its moisture to her heart and won
Ease from the first day's burning sun;
Lord of the pomp a crown endows
And peoples hail on kingly brows;
Lord of the beggar's tattered coat,
A derelict on life's sea a-float;
Lord of thy blinded children, they —
Who see no sunlight in the day,
Nor star-shine in the night — but be
Dreamless toilers on land and sea;
Lord, Very God of these works of thine,
Hear me, I beseech thee, most divine!
Lord I praise thee, and adore thee
For thy great works laid before me.
My prayer-book is thine open air
Where nature prints thy Laws so clear;

My altar is the human strife
Where I take sacraments of life;
My proof in immortality
Speaks loud in every blossoming tree.
Lord, Very God, now lift I my voice
Thanking thee for that which I rejoice —
Thy gift of life, be it short or long,
And with it the great gift of song!